Preface

*   Back Ground Story

Index

*   Goals & Dreams
*   Economy Plan
*   What's Pluto?
*   What Ramel needs to be happy "Greed"
*   Motivation
*   Collaborate
*   Real Estate
*   Jehovah Test
*   Relaxation
*   CSH
*   Religious Belief
*   Business
*   Mental Illness Movie
*   Risk Factors and how to Manage them
*   Hospital CSH & ESH gradual release process phases
*   Elaborate on experiences at CSH
*   Progress
*   Trust   Hope
*   Good Fellows
*   Random
*   Logo's
*   Manage a mental illness
*   Supernatural
*   Headings for " PLUTO"
*   What do I want to be?
*   Insurances: Progressive
*   Sinnz = Icon = PLUTO

*   Goals
*   Equal Power
*   Balance Power
*   Jehovah?
*   Membership With "PLUTO"
*   Statement
*   Program
*   Religious Belief Elaborated
*   PLUTO jingle
*   PLUTO's education collaboration program
*   PLUTO entertainment program
*   PLUTO medical care program
*   PLUTO Majette fashion program network
*   PLUTO Bank program
*   PLUTO Associate connection society
*   PLUTO Individual Help service program
*   Members making money once a member on the website
*   Planet Pluto World invest in Theme Parks
*   PLUTO's calendar schedule program
*   SkinZone Manufacturing
*   PLUTO's federal talk program
*   PLUTO's individual classification profile
*   Constructing PLUTO's network
*   Qualifications to be a member
*   Public sources
*   Write how risk factors have effected you Ramel in the past, then write how you Ramel will manage risk factors in the future

*   Upgrades Process Program on PLUTO
*   Everybody's ideas get noticed on PLUTO
*   PLUTO
*   PLUTO's biblica
*   Conclusion

Chapter 1

Background Story- Preface

As a kid I always had big dreams, like becoming a football player, actor or even a doctor. I always wondered what my future would hold. I was born in Hampton, Virginia on 2/26/93. I moved to Brooklyn, New York when I was three months old. I remember having a father and a mother,a brother named Patrick, several cousins, aunts and uncles. I called my nana "Mrs. Puzo".

My brother had serious temper tantrums. My family couldn't take him anywhere, he would purely embarrass everybody. His behavior was so corrupt he had to take medication and attend special schools. My brother's intentions were good, but he had a problem. Saying all this is not for you to dislike my brother it's just to let you know as we got older the tables turned. Eventually my brother got better but I developed a mental illness.

Now I'm the one taking medication, acting bizarre in public and embarrassing people in my family. I lived in Brooklyn, New York for seven years and found out that the man who raised me and who I knew as my father wasn't really my father. That phase in my life really stained me. I literally cried for two years, and didn't feel right with my mom being with any other man but him.

In 2000, my mom and brother and I left New York and moved to Newport News, Virginia. I was seven, my brother was six. Living in Newport News, you had to grow up on your own, fast. You have gangs, street life, and bullies. In the third grade I remember being beat up everyday by a kid named Dywane. As soon as I walked in my classroom he'd have his fist pounding against his hand and he would grab me then throw me in the desk, punch me multiple times in the head, and he'd continue until the teacher came in the classroom.

Tired of the abuse, I fought back one day when he tripped me walking to the buses. I ran up to him and started hitting him in the head. His friend "Derek" broke it up. We caught the bus and went home. The next day Derek came up to me and asked how I felt about the fight I bragged a little and said I whooped his ass and I could beat him up again if we fought again.

Derek got the word and told Dywane. Dywane was pissed. When I walked in the classroom the next morning he grabbed me by the shoulders and threw me into the desk, and ramming me into chairs and tables. All the kids in the classroom just watched and stared.

This time when I went home I told my mom what happened. We drove into the neighborhood where Dywane lived and we saw him and asked to talk to his mother. The next day I was scared to go to school but I had to go anyway. My mother always said "if you don't go to school you'll become a bum," so I stepped in the class. From that day, Dywane started calling me his brother.

Growing up in Newport News I witnessed the strangest people. When I lived in Regency Square Apartments there was a man named "Hustle Man". He would literally go through the dumpster like he was searching for hidden treasure. My family also went through a tough time. We got evicted and then we lived with another family. My brother, my mother, and I lived in the smallest bedroom of their home. My brother and I slept on the floor and my mom slept in a twin bed. My mom was working at 7-11 at the time and had all types of guys interested in her. There was one man who bought her an Explorer and a two bedroom apartment in Denbigh, Newport News. His name was Willy Randall. My family and I moved in with Mr. Randall. Growing up in N.N. I was introduced to gangs, drugs, and violence. I met this guy Ronzel in school and he persuaded me to join this gang called A.C.E. I told him to bring his crew to my house so I could join in or, in other words "come home." After school, I saw him and his friends walking up the street getting ready to knock on my door. I was paranoid as hell because, to join a gang you have to get "jumped in". So, I heard a knock on my door and followed them out back to the swing set.

There were four of them, and one was holding a camera. They triangled me. One man hit me from the side and I swung at E-dot, the leader of the group. They all attacked me left and right until I burst into tears. They stopped after 3 minutes and threw a black bandana on me and walked off, looking at the camera. I went back home and put ice on my face and sat in my room until I fell asleep.

While I was in a gang I involved myself with stealing cars, robbing people, and doing drugs. I felt like I was growing up too fast and was headed in the wrong direction. Learning these trades, I realized I was too paranoid to continue with these behaviors, so I stayed in the house and went to school. In 2008, my uncle died. From then on, I retaliated by hanging out with the wrong group of people. When my mother saw her family breaking apart she moved from Newport News to Yorktown, Virginia.

Being a new kid in a different town and my uncle's death, enraged me, so I started doing drugs and committed armed robbery. My mom found out I was doing drugs so she started a curfew time for me to come in the house. When I disobeyed her rules she locked me out of the house. I used to get so angry and would kick on her door until she let me in. One day it got so bad I took a 2x4 piece of wood and smashed a hole in her wall. She immediately called the police and I went to Merrimac Detention Center.

When I got out I discovered most of the people I was hanging out with either died or went to jail for a long time. Even E-dot died. **RIP.** When I got out I was placed on house arrest but, I didn't like the rules. I broke them and got locked up again. Being in Merrimac and the frustration I had caused conflict on every ward. The only ward they could send me to was the female ward. I had fun on that ward and maintained good behavior. After my time was up I was sent home again on house arrest. I hated the rules, and got in trouble and locked up again. This time when I was released the courts sent me to Crossroads, a group home facility.

Crossroads Group Home was where I had to do a whole lot of growing up with high authority, similar to Eastern State and Central State. My first day there, Mr. Washington, Mr. Cocea, and the supervisor of the group home addressed me to my room. After lunch we went to go see a semi-pro team The Norfolk Tides. Later that day, I found out they gave the group home free tickets every once in a while. I felt Norfolk Tides sympathy for us later on I envision Pluto and co-owning Norfolk Tides some day and changing their name to Virginia Tidewaters. This is a great idea because Virginia, has no professional team besides the Washington Redskins in the District of Columbia. Norfolk is part of the seven cities a.k.a Tidewater Area. Why not call Norfolk Tides, The Virginia Tidewaters?

I matured a lot at Crossroads under the authority of staff. They would make sure I woke up on time, specifically military style. Living independently and responsibly on my own without parents and living in a structured facility with peers I could relate to. Growing up with these peers, you see people who make it and people who don't make it living under the rules in the facility. You get to learn the different background stories people have when they get locked up. I used to wonder how other black juveniles will make it through the system like me.

I will never forget the experiences I had in Crossroads. I experienced my roommate hanging himself, doing other gateway drugs and escaping with three other residents. The tragic death experience of my roommate hanging himself was one hell of an experience. I remember Austin would write in his journal every day. He'd write all day and night until he'd go to bed and I used to wonder what he was writing about. And when he passed away he was writing about his Good-Byes. **RIP**

Meeting different residents that come through the group home, I really learned a lot about people and their character. By their character, I mean where they came from, what they've been into and what drugs they do. I used to try gateway drugs other then marijuana, such as pills and huffing. These drugs influenced my knowledge about drugs and what the trip is.

One day at the group home, one of the residents came back drunk. I was angry because my mom told on me once for getting drunk on a home visit. I wanted to run away so I could tear into my mom. Montray, the resident who was drunk, got into an argument with staff. Another resident, Brandon Anderson, was angry this day so we all went with my plan to run away that night. I went back into my room and packed up some clothes. All three of us headed out into some double doors. We first ran straight to the train tracks and kept going until we saw a train headed in our direction. We spied our first train and hopped on the side of the tracks. Montray yelled "cover your eyes and ears". I asked "why" he said "it's too fast". So we got off the train tracks and walked to McDonalds, and headed to the hotel across the street. My friends called their parents and regretted running away. The clerk said "where's your room, you're going to have to do something with your bags". So we left and walked to 7-11 down the street and used their pay phone. Out of nowhere cop cars surrounded us, we ran to the back of 7-11. Two of us fell, tumbling down the ditch. I got up and ran toward the train tracks and hid in the bushes. After waiting for clearance, I went looking for my friends. After walking down the train tracks I found Brandon Anderson. He whispered "is the coast clear?" I said "yea". He came out of the bushes and we both wondered where Montray was. We couldn't find him. It was just me and Brandon hiding from the cops.

We got off the train tracks and walked on a road with a corn field. This road was dark, a few cars passed us and it was foggy. The road led us back to the store and the police spotted us and surrounded us. The police got out with their weapons and asked why we ran, they asked for our social security numbers etc. The police knew we were from Crossroads. The director Mr. Wallace, said "lock us up." Next we headed back to Merrimac Detention Center and were evaluated. Montray came and we wondered where he went. He said he went back to Crossroads. We asked "damn how did you run so fast?" After the evaluation we went to our wards.

I saw familiar faces, staff said "you're back again, and brought two more with you this time Majette." They split us up on different wards. Montray and Brandon went to Ward 4 and I went to Ward 3. We all were curious about each other's court dates. Montray's was first and the court sent him back to Crossroads. Then was Brandon and the court sent him home. When it was my turn, the court told me I had to do the Post-D residential program at the detention center. I finished the program less than six months and came out while I was in the 12th grade.

CHAPTER TWO

Close to the end of my last semester of school, I developed a chemical imbalance in my brain. So one day I got out off of school and bought some weed. I chilled with both my boys. Towards the end of the day it was just me and my brother chilling and smoking on his bed. Out of nowhere I started hearing repeated voices telling me take my step-dad's car keys and "drive...drive...drive." The voices commanded me to do so. So, I asked my brother if he wanted to go for a ride. He said "yea" I crept upstairs and the keys were on my mom's dresser. I took them. I went back to my brother's room and said, "I have the keys are you ready?!" He said, "I was just playing." I headed out the door without him.

So, I went to the vehicle and unlocked the door and thought about the crazy stuff I was hearing in my head. "You're going to have to learn one day, this is only your first time learning on your own." So, hearing those true voices about myself I started up the ignition and put the gear in reverse and started driving down my neighborhood and back to my driveway. I was satisfied about how far I drove so I took the keys out of the ignition. And again the voices came back while I was sitting in the driver's seat. I was ready to go back into the house. The voices repeatedly said, "Ramel drive, drive, drive on the main road." I thought to myself "it's just my first time why not?!" So, I started up the ignition and headed for the main road.

Driving on the main road and not in my right state of mind, I was able to control the car physically but not mentally. The road was like a big hallucination, visual, hearing commanding thoughts all at the same time. I heard commands "turn left on this street and turn right on this street." It was terrible. So listening to the voices I ended up on Ironbound Road. The same road Eastern State is on in Williamsburg, Virginia. So while I'm driving on Ironbound Road, an all black police car flashed his lights on my vehicle. I pulled the car over. While I'm pulling the car over I can't see anything out the windshield. The cop blinded me. So, having my right foot on the brakes while not seeing anything, I accidently crashed the car into a utility pole. The air bags deployed on me. My body went into shock. So after the crash, I jumped out of the car and put my hands up, saying to the officer "I will serve my consequences." The officer said he pulled me over for a broken tail light and he gave me a breathalyzer test. I blew out 00.00 so then the officer asked for my license and registration that I didn't have. So, he called for backup and the towing company. I remembered I brought the weed with me. I stashed it in the glove compartment. I was hoping when back up came they wouldn't make the decision to search the car. Back up pulled up and the tow truck came behind them because the airbags deployed. Since I didn't have a license or registration, they were able to search the vehicle. I was like "damn" smoking on a cigarette. As I was watching them search the car, I was like "why the voices ain't talking to me now?" This night, to me, was meant to happen. All I can say in my head, that it was my first time stealing the car. I was

7

lying down on the pavement when they said, "we found something." It was my bag of marijuana that I'd bought earlier. They arrested me and all I could do was think about how I was just about to graduate from high school. I had SOL's and examines to study for.

Now, I'm at jail, the officer and CO took my mug shot and scanned my finger tips. Now it was time to see the magistrate. All he did was look at me and said "I was young and dumb." He let me go on a bond. I wondered who was going to take me home. The C.O. talked to the officer who pulled me over and persuaded him to take me home because I was only 18.I ended up getting a ride back from the officer who made me total my parent's car. He had my bag of marijuana in his glove compartment. I wanted that bag of weed too. We got to my house and my step-father answered the door and asked "what the hell happened to my car?" The officer explained the situation and came to the conclusion that he blind sighted me, so it wasn't my fault that the car crashed. So, the officer and my step-dad exchanged insurance companies. My mom came down the stairs and explained that she was really disappointed in me. She was like "you got a second chance" and that just reminded me about school.

So, the following day of school I was so determined to succeed that I passed all my exams and SOL's and on graduation day, I marched right across that stage. I felt like Jehovah as my life was with me from the beginning.

PLANET PLUTO WORLD

Schizoaffective Vision
By Ramel Majette

Goals and Dreams –

Name of the organization is "Pluto". My name is Ramel Majette, the creator of all of this. My ambition is to become a barber, producer, franchise, investor ultimate money maker around the world, and a boss. I feel like, I'll finally enjoy life and make ultimate dreams come true on Earth for people.

When I was young in my teenage years, I got in trouble with the law a lot. So I got sent to this group home. My first day there, we went out to go see semi-pro team, Norfolk VA Tides. Later on that day I found out they gave us free tickets every month and I felt their heart. So, I had this vision that one day I want to own them and make them pro and name them Virginia Tidewaters. Symbol I think the name is cool because the Tidewater area in Virginia is the seven cities where I'm from.

"Pluto" world wants to focus on producing the best produce, like fruits, veggies, plants, organic resources herbs and pottery. Products like these needs to be produced more and sold cheaply to people.

I'd like to own a clothing line a clothing line named "Ink Elephant." Comfortable polo shirts in my particular design and cargo shorts and shoes. Right now, I'm in CSH,but when I get out I want to finish my barber license.I refuse to be a nobody.

Economy Plan –

When I do well with my barbering career I'd like to own a detailed studio. I'll find people who with talent in making music in my favorite genre "classical, hip hop, rap, R&B, rock and pop".

I know for sure the best source of energy is the sun. In fact, the sun energy is infinity and solar energy manipulates that source. Mr. Brown a tech from CSH if he was in power he would put solar panels on top of peoples homes, apartments homes and large businesses to save utility money. That's what PLUTO wants to see happen. Imagine if Americans didn't have to pay Dominion Power ½ as much or 25 % as much as they charge. It's a conservative idea for the Economy. People like Mr. Brown have brilliant ideas to manipulate solar panels to save money for families.

What's "Pluto"? –

Pluto is the planet farthest from the sun and now it's an ice cap. Me = Ramel Majette has this idea to fiction break this ice cap and bring Pluto on Earth, since this is fiction broken and birth on earth. I'm going to make Planet Pluto World into a network on the internet. Pluto World focuses on everything I previously wrote and what I'm going to continue to write.

What's Ramel need to be happy "Greed" –

Materialism is the number one gift to mankind. Everybody wants it all. Infinity to modern day phones and computers to modern day cars and trucks. People that can't afford such things stress and will do anything willing to get a modern day car or phone. Pluto wants to help make a difference. I know greed is a sign of evil, but I would be happy if I had the necessary things in life and didn't have any stress about losing them. I will give anything I don't want or need to individual people who are in poverty hand to hand and give them a source for help for food and living. That's Pluto all about sources.

Motivation –

Determination is where it starts. When the determination switch turns on in your head you start to fight obstacles. Don't fight them too hard, take your time at doing them, and have faith. My faith is that I believe in Jehovah the Father of Jesus Christ, living for the love of what you're doing increases your interest and your motivation.

Collaborate –

Collaboration is where connection comes in handy. Friends or associates are the main source to get in touch with invitation to events. Working together as a team that's collaborating. I know for sure collaborating all businesses around the world and subjecting them in different genre and classified them in an organization. Businesses will start individually take control of their city instead of stressing out on how much taxes or money they owe the government.

Real-Estate –

First I have to start from the bottom like selling trailers, RV's houses, apartment complex's. Then money will be inevitable "master salesman". I'll use the best, funniest, and intellectual advertising a high functioning real estate business "PLUTO Wants to Succeed". Once I accomplish these goals, I'll make a difference.

Jehovah Test –

Content of character, personality and looks is how God made us all different. Sense of Humor is where we find talent in people and wisdom is good to keep, but how can we pass Jehovah test? Which is honesty? I know you have to be true to yourself. I'm different I'm in my zone "PLUTO". I'll hire mental health stable employees. Why because I have a mental issue and everybody's needs a chance.

Relaxation –

"ICU" Intensive Care Unit, hydroponic marijuana, exotic marijuana, and medicate marijuana needs to be legal and run by the government. Massage from therapist is relaxing but trust issues are stressful. If things are not right you fix, recycle, refresh, renew and use. My mom Elaine Majette is a massage therapist and she owns a product line called "Skin Zone" and she needs her own empire.

CSH – Central State Hospital

Is a forensic hospital I mean the only maximum security forensic hospital in the state of Virginia and that's where I'm at now. People come here if they have mental issues. For example people with psychosis. Here they have different diagnosis and different stories behind them that lead them up in here. The daily activities we do at CHS is we wake up, do hygiene, take meds at specific times and go to treatment mall which is like an alternative school for patients. People here are not crazy, weird or have no reason to be on Earth, they just have a beautiful mind.

Religious Belief –

I use to say I was a Jehovah Witness, but it didn't make sense witnessing Jehovah so I came up with this new faith called Jehovah Believers, it's just makes way more sense to me. My guess, believing in Jehovah everything will work out with your health, freedom, achievements and success. Then exiting out of that struggle, then enjoy life. Tour through states, rivers, lakes, oceans…and one of my dreams go to continent Africa. I believe sticking to my faith this will come true for me and fulfill my goals with which is to build the PLUTO empire and I'm the emperor.

Businesses –

I'll like to one day own a "Finance Company", (A company that makes short term loans usually to individuals). When I own a company like, then I will be helping people in desperate need. Especially, if they're about to lose their home, car, or need for food. I would like to acquire a franchise license, with that I can own franchise companies across the world. Financial Empire Wealth is on my mind. Building a Majesty- Sovereign Power Authority or dignity, this is the definition about living royal. I pray to Jehovah to grant my wish and follow the Messiah words King of the Jews, (Jesus expected deliverer to make Pluto Records come true). Sun unlimited energy.

Mental Illness Movie –

Trying to make "Pluto" is the theme. Learn as much as you can about Mental Illness and medication. How to treat patients over time. With honesty to listen and comprehend in the right state of mind. My experience with mental illness has been a trip to hospitalization, going through episodes, and repeating the process of mental health treatment. Seeing different patients when your hospitalized you witness different diagnosis and how that person personality changes, is something you'll never forget.

My achievements that I learned are to take my meds everyday at specific times and learn about my phases which are triggers, early warning signs, symptoms and how to manage symptoms. Learning my risk factors and how to manage risk factors.

My success in CSH is going to the canteen, keeping a job in the canteen, making level 3 on my daily point sheet at the end of each day and continuing the process. Pursuing "Good behavior", so I can transfer to a civil hospital. Exit

Risk Factors and How to Manage Them –
1) Major Mental Illness (Schizoaffective Disorder, Bipolar Type):
    Triggers, Early warning signs, symptoms, and how to manage symptoms.
2) Threat Control Override symptoms: Take medication, trust family members advice and Doctor advice.
3) Substance Abuse: AA, NA sessions, stay away from influences, relax therapy and a support system.
4) Aggression/dangerous to others: Walk away and use coping skills, relax yoga techniques.
5) Personality Disorder/Traits (Anti-Social): Continue with therapy.
6) Denial / Lack of Insight: Learn about the mental illness and how it affects me.
7) Non-compliance with treatment and/or medication: Continue with medication treatment.
8) Psychosocial/Family issues: Family Therapy and support group.
9) Suicide/Self Injury: Think about the beauty of life, and love for myself, take medication, and call crisis line and police when I'm in harm.
10) Non-Violent Criminal Behavior: No wrong choices in life.
11) Employment/Daytime Activity upon conditional release: go to school, "College", and get a job.
12) Demo-graphic/Statistic Factor: Positive Association and make good choices.

Hospital "CSH" and "ESH" Gradual Release Process Phases –
1) Civil Transfer
2) Escorted Grounds
3) Unescorted Grounds
4) Escorted Community
5) Unescorted Community 8hrs
6) Unescorted Community 48 hrs
7) Conditional and Unconditional Release

STUDY!!

Elaborate on experiences in "CSH" –

- I've been in restraints several different times with injections shot to the ass cheeks.
- I spent 3 nights in the seclusion room before.
- I heard voices to throw everything away, special cards from my family and my friends.
- Cursed out staff and threw chairs around the ward.
- Got committed and had to go through the gradual process.
- Experience Stepdad "Willie Randall" died.
- Went into numerous episodes, like got naked and walked down the hallway because of voices.
- I've done 500 piece puzzles and 1000 piece puzzles.
- Got into fights with staff battling to break us up.
- Threw tables.
- Had relationships with females.
- "Treatment Mall" classes you take during the week days.
- "Mrs. Coleman" my personal therapist.
- Treatment Team with Dr. Tidler, Dr. Riley, Mrs. Pierce, Mr. Grimes and Mr. Gyur.
- Take medication at specific times: morning, noon and night.
- Holiday Parties, Bingo, Games and winning prizes.
- Listening to radio music and dancing.
- Working in the canteen, boss Ms. Harris.

Progress –

GROW !!

KNOWLEDGE!!

BELIEVE!!

TEAMWORK!!

ACCUMULATE!!

Trust Hope –

Five words that describe me: Determined, Hopeful, Clean, Dreamful, Never Giving Up. Do I really want to stay away from marijuana? No, but I have to. Pros to stop using: Meds, Conditional Release, Staying out of Trouble, Being a positive role model. It's illegal in this state and bad for my health. Cons to continue use: relax me, fun, motivates me to make money, want more out of life, and have fun with everything I do. It helps me cope with myself and my innerbeing.

Good fellas-

Accept

People

For

Who

They

Are!!

Random –
Kings, Goals, Accomplishments, Win, Queens, City and Castle!!!
Love – Happy, Giving – Money, Unique – Different*

Logos –
"Patient is a virtue"   "Work hard"   "Play hard"   "Courage"
"Active Power to Accomplish" "Go Get It" "Brave" "Moral Excellence"
"Money Talks Bullshit Walks" "Communication" "Cars and Trucks" "Dr. Majette" "Live within your means" "Driving" "Flowers" "Fox" "Air Balloon" "PLUTO"
Logos –
"Started from the bottom Now we here"   "Have a Purpose" "Your own style flavor" "True to yourself" "Never giving up hope" "Solve Issues" "Never perfect but possible to be smarter" "Find your own talent"
Logos –
"Being funny" "Rejuvenating the Soul" "Want better things in Life" "Never giving up" "Enlightment" "The sky is the limit"

Managing a Mental Illness –
Trigger: Stress, depression, boredom, and nothing productive in life. Warning signs: Less sleep, irrational thoughts, racing thoughts, and whispers.

Symptoms: Hallucinations, delusions, manic positive behavior, religious belief out of control, and not sleeping.
How to manage symptoms: Take medication; continue therapy with Dr. and counselors, and case managers.
Supernatural -
"Pluto" is going to be a form in to a power or a spirit like satin, Jehovah and Jesus the Son. People are going to say "I need PLUTO", like the saying "I need Jesus". From birth and ground zero, my name was Ramel Majette Isiah. I'm going to create my second name to Dr. Majette. Prague Clock: Is a mid-evil astronomical clock located in Prague the capitol of the Czech Republic. The clock was first installed in 1410 making it the 3rd oldest astronomical clock in the world and the oldest one still working. Mounted on the southern wall on Old Towne City Hall in the Old Towne Square. Clock maker Mikulas of Kadan and Jan Sindel, the latter professor of mathematics and astronomy at Charles University celebrated 1600 anniversary October 9, 2010.

"Planet PLUTO Is Here to Help the People and Unite Americans Around the Universe".

"Excel to Perfection" "Diversity" "Opportunity" "Jobs" "Job Titles" "Royal Life" "Employment" Patrick Majette Songwriter.

What Do I Want To Be? –
"Doctor" "Producer" "Investor" "Boss" "Real Estate" www.pluto "Director"
"Owner" "Designer" "Barber" "Writer" "Artist" "Astronomer" "Astronaut"

Insurance: Progressive -
"Cars" "Bikes" "House" "Health" "Job" "Dental" "Medical" "Boat" "Phone" "Life"
"Bills" "Children" "Family" "Businesses" "Banks" "Real Estate" "Land" "Production"

SINNZ = ICON =PLUTO –
"A.C.E. = Associates Conquer Earth -
Sinners become better people and change negative actions and decisions making in their lives.

Pg. 24   (see photo that should be added) = stands for Sinnz

*Goals –
"Demand the Best" " Clear Vision"
"Committed 2 Excellence"
"Real Friends" "Common Sense"
"Dictionary" "Foundation"

Skin Zone, Barbering
Producing Studio   Girl Friends
     PLUTO

Cars	Entertainment
Jewelry	Clothes
Show Out	Shoes/Hats

Homes in different states:
Florida, New York, Virginia, and California.

** Sun Energy **

*Equalpower –

King = Ramel

Jehovah = PLUTO

Jesus = Sinnz

Queens = Angels

** Media
&
Gossip/Politics
Evil = A.C.E.

*Balance Power –

www.PlanetPLUTO: Necessary for the people, you work for, a growing organization industry.

Father Jehovah = Ramel's Life
Son Jesus = Ramel's blood

Evil Satan = Ramel's Father

Jesus died for our sins. Jehovah's the creator and Satan is the thief.

My blood sustained, my father dies, and my life continues.
Draw scale into the following:

United   Power
A.C.E.   Associates, Conquer, Earth

A Work Association
Jehovah? –

What's a Prince
2 A King
What's a King
2 A God

What's a God
2 A Non – Believer?

Draw clouds below

Question God   Answer Me

Membership with "PLUTO" –

First you have to sign and fill out an application contract on the web-site. This is contracted by A.C.E.. If you submit the contract you're automatically an A.C.E Associate. Why? Because we are all sinners and associates on this network.

Second, you find a job you're interested in and expand your ideas, and then you set up an online store selling SkinZone Manufacturing Products.

Third, after you're comfortable and stable with the program industry you start exploring new routes and get involved with the connections and the everlasting progress in your life.

Statement –

PLUTO IS A LIFE CARE THAT BENEFITS!

Program –

Fantasy Ideas - for "Pluto": www.Pluto.net is an Industry Membership life care business, infinity entertainment that's enjoyable. Log on to this website and it can help you to anything to meet your needs. Example: If you need a car, job or shelter its handed to you if your membership is approved. Once you're part of the membership you are welcome to "PLANET PLUTO WORLD". You will have no stress, unlimited fun and a work program that is best fit for an individual. How? We unite as many manufacturing businesses around the world and collaborate it with SkinZone Incorporate. Reality Ideas for Pluto Foundation: Get my barber license, own my own barber shop, build my studio and invest in my mom's product line Skinzone. Make "Associates Conquer Earth" Membership = A positive association that's a strong workforce and is a "Family Hood United Kingdom". "PLUTO"

Program –

Fantasy Ideas - for "PLUTO" www.PLUTO.com network is a classified website that's a business for A.C.E. and an immediate connection to resources. "PLANET PLUTO WORLD BUILDING", is a work organization focused on reaching out to new people, small businesses and large businesses, different countries and cities. Then try to ask people if they want to try the organization, "Family hood United Kingdom". PLUTO DREAMS is to one day unite all the hospitals around the world. New medications and break through cures will be known and information will be passed through quickly. PLUTO invented this chain reaction and is determined to work hard till it's finished. Members are qualified for health care, life care, medical care and at the very least access to members to associates that have been with the program up to 5 years. Reality Ideas - for "PLUTO": Sign back up for SSI, disability and social security for money support, and get my driver's license. I would like to finance a Dodge Dart II or Chevy Truck and be true to myself and receive honest feedback from other associates.

"PLUTO", is a business that the people can control such as, health care, insurance protection, and work force, instead of the government. The Government controls the military and the legal system. The advantages of "PLANET PLUTO WORLD" re-enacting on earth. This is power for the people and not for the media, politics or Government. "We can fight for fairness".

Religious Belief Elaborated –
Jehovah my life, the reason I say this "Jehovah my life" because I gave him a higher position in my life then just my father. I don't know my biological father, he is not existing in my life right now. That's why I previously balance Him as my life, because my life continues.

Jesus MY Blood: Jesus died for our sins and he shed his blood and body. In church we practice communion which is grape juice representing Jesus' blood and a cracker representing Jesus' body remembering he died for our sins. I feel like since I practice that ritual I can say Jesus is within me, "My blood".

Satan My Father: Satin is a thief and Jehovah is our heavenly father. Satan wants to still anything Jehovah creates or does, true indeed. So I gave Satan the position as my Father, he won't have to steal another one. Every father figure I had either died or left my life. But, I don't know my biological father. He doesn't exist.

I mixed the supernatural with my writing because I'm confused about a lot of stuff. I'm schizoaffective bi-polar type. Which is a mental illness I suffer from and it makes me curious about stuff like this. Don't take what I wrote for certain, it's some that's true and some that's put in my own interpretation, "it satisfies me".

Jingle for PLUTO –

WE ARE ALL PEOPLE,
HUMAN BEINGS WITH DREAMS
AND WITH PLUTO IN YOUR LIFE
YOU CAN BE IN THAT SCENE"

Pluto's Education Collaboration Program-
Planet Pluto World Associates can live their dream because with the family hood PLUTO produced associates to help one another to progress in their lives. If you're a member then we waste no time on making each individual goals come true. The goal has to be positive for the economy, productive to keep people busy, and constructive so everyone is happy working. Every associate common goal is to own nice homes in peaceful neighborhoods, drive fancy cars, live important and happy in each individual life. "PLUTO" wants to make those options easily handed to my members. Because nothing in life should be stressful, on earth we have the ability to do what's right and solve statistics. In criminal acts people cause it to be so high, the root starts from not having wants and needs. So, www.planetplutoworld.network/com is the source to put heaven on earth. Constructing this network needs to include a "Search Engine", "Federal Talk" (Associates Gossip Connection Media), and our "People Service" (Professionals that hold important information about the industry). "PLUTO" is A manufacturing money

laundering professional organization. The Program invests in Premium quality in all merchandise and sells it for a discount. Producing PLUTO records: Hip Hop, R&B, Rap, Pop, and Classical Music are the genre. Build studio from the ground up and learn how to make beats and fine talented artist. Record label name "PLANET PLUTO WORLD INC." Become a music movie director to entertain the world.

PLUTO'S Entertainment Program –

PLUTO'S Entertainment Program is where the dream process comes true in this network. How? As a member you are connected to this big entrepreneur organization that wants to expand its empire. With this achievement people can see, play in scenes and act with their favorite people. Entertainment sources like television shows, movies, concerts and plays.

PLUTO Medical Care Program –

PLUTO Medical Care Program is a blessing to us all. Money is always funded in A.C.E Association. So as a member your insurance policy is always covered with our "A.C.E Association Organization Network". Planet Pluto World focus on uniting insurance companies and policies because the more connections the better the transaction for health care medical care. Insurance Companies need a battle ground source from the people. So they will not have the same excuse that individuals who do not have enough money for hospital benefits.

JHON Q.

PLUTO Majette Fashion Network –

Majette Fashion line can open doors for any individual who likes to create shirts, shoes, hats, belts, jewelry, etc. As long as you are a member of the A.C.E Association and filled out an application on the website, nobody's ideas get ignored. Once the associate displays his or her idea they get looked at on the website. Then viewers look and judge your creativity. If its "liked" then your mailbox will receive messages with feedback and then you illustrate your product and send it to PLUTO Manufacturing. It will get factored then sold on the market. Each Associates creation gets 40% profit back, they create and is sold . Other fashion companies can be a member of Majette fashion line too. We will unite upgrade and progress. We manufacture together with this achievements, associates can choose which line they want to work with.

PLUTO Bank Program –

Pluto only deals with Federal Credit Unions. So every member who is approved will have a bank account with a local credit union. Why the organization only deals with credit unions? Because Credit Unions are Federal and PLUTO trust credit unions. Federal Credit unions will be asked to be part of www.Planet Pluto World.com   (suns photo) MONOPOLY (suns photo).

PLUTO Associates Connection Society –

With the A.C.E. Association "Federal Talk" program on the website. People can find individuals that been through professions or educational systems that Associates interest in that person. Then receive information on what it takes to get a specific job title. Members receive grants from the organization to help them with their education. With this organization grant, the pressure for you to start and finish is a must. You can have access to any school equipment, technology or tutor for support. Features on the website are "Stock Society": where you can set up your own website store to buy invest and sell merchandise to make money. "Education Society": is access to any school source across the world, and each school selection you pick has detailed information you can look for. "Work Force Society". As an A.C.E. member on the website your connected with small businesses and large businesses in your Community. Eventually, "PLUTO's": members always has a good reference to find valuable jobs for associates.

***FRANCHISE COMPANIES ***
PLUTO INDIVIDUAL HELP SERVICE PROGRAM -

If a member needs help with any of the following schools/education, job or transportation etc. The A.C.E Associates is a family hood network, so we look out for one another like a family does. PLUTO is a good network and a Prime Minister who only wants the best for each associate, and it's a promise! *Members Making Money Wants a Member on the Website* - Once you're done with our application and finished setting up the "class profile". You are now welcome the "Genre Selection of Societies" - Which is different selection of programs or apps. The main source to connect for income is "Stock Society": where you can set-up your own website store and buy and invest merchandise to make income.

*" Planet Pluto World" * Invest in theme parks - Busch Gardens, Water Country, Six Flags, Kings Dominion, Disney World/Land, Sea World, and etc.

JANUARY : People will have to make

profiles this month because it's the only month, you can make your profile and join as a Member. But for the first five years "PLUTO" is introduced to the world. People will have yearly to join as a member.

FEBUARY: You look for your career goal and ask

how to get involved by clicking on "People Service". Getting in touch with your interest is first with "PLUTO" policy.

March : In this month every new member will be introduced to

*Skinzone Manufacturing. * Which is part of the network and is the main factor on "Stock Society". When introduced to Skinzone Manfacturing you'll be asked to set-up your own web-site store and sale products. Each worker will get an income for how many products they sale.

April : Associates get started on something constructive and productive.

"PLUTO's" policy wants to make sure every associate is getting involved with the network and expanding it with progress and brilliant creative ideas. If already, just have fun exploring.

May:

People should be progressing everyday while involved with the network. So, saving money shouldn't be a hassle, or if a hassle click on *Peoples Service* and will provide you with your own personal *Budgeting Buddy*. This is the beginning of beautiful weather and upcoming events are coming up so be warned!

June:

Tickets! Tickets! Tickets! Discounts! Discounts! Tickets and Discounts! A beautiful combination all summer long tickets to theme parks, concerts, shows play acts, and etc. all summer long. "PLUTO" focus on fun but business is always first so your personal phone is how you will keep up with the latest data on your website store. Easy!

July:

Fresh ideas for advertising "Planet Pluto World" from associates. New Advertisements will be created by the members that work in "Planet Pluto World Building". Good and Funny, Intelligent advertising for "Planet Pluto World". Advertisements must be created during this time. Because football season is coming up and it had been six months since you can sign up with the industry.

August :

All associates work hard, play hard, and continue on making money and saving money. Continue on progressing with your education plan and support is granted whenever you need it.

September:

Football season starts!! Tickets are being sold on the website, if possible discounts. Members will be asked on a 3 month tour to advertise "PLUTO".

October:

Trip Plans to travel around the world looking and introducing to new people about "PLUTO".   We travel to different countries, cities, islands and carribean expanding our network. If for any reason associates can't join the adventure there's always next year.

November:

Cruises, Tours, and expanding the network everyday. Phone's to keep up with data from website store business.

December:

Back from cruises and tours.   No Holiday stress.

SkinZone Manufacturing -

SkinZone is a product line created by "Elaine Majette".   It's organic, tropical nuts, that have been extracted into body butter. This product is healthy for the skin, make you look much younger then before and ten times better then oil and grease products. SkinZone product line sells a variety of body butters, body cream, shampoo, conditioner, bath salts, lotion, hair care products and etc.   SkinZone product line will be a branch in "SkinZone Manufacturing". SkinZone Manufacturing is a manufacturing business only manufacturing nothing but skincare products. Other then "Pluto Manufacturing" sells nothing but premium merchandise. These two manufactures are the only stock where you can invest, buy and sell on "Stock Society" and progress on your web-site store. "PLUTO's" Focus on uniting other manufacturing business and making them a source on the network.

Draw a picture of the world.   *****

"PLUTO" Federal Talk Program -

" Federal Talk" is another Icon on the web-site. Clicking on the Icon opens up the social media part of the network.   This will be one of the most important tools on the network. Why? With this base social media A.C.E. associates can update events have conversation with another member, report local new, report and get members on a community support project. And most important criticize politicians and help economy growth. Home videos can be made and uploaded. Videos have to be appropriate.

"PLUTO" Individual Classification Profile –

This is basically your profile. But with numerous of classifiers , because of the expansion of the network. As you go on and explore through the network and save and collect items. Your "ICP" Individual Classification Profiles, will automatically organize and save it for you in your profile. You'll receive this after filling and submitting the application after signing up.

Constructing Pluto Network –

"Planet PLUTO World" website needs a team of website designer, computer techs and motivating people from everywhere across the globe to get involved with this network. Building my vision of what Planet PLUTO World should look like is increasingly the word "grandiose". But "Hey" with my plans with the A.C.E (Associates Conquer Earth), associates everywhere have the chance to be grandiosity.   It will take funded money from people who wants to invest in" Planet PLUTO World" and volunteer help.

Qualifications to be a member –

Member has to be 14 yrs. of age with plenty of goals and dreams they want to pursuit in life.   Willing to commit to a membership A.C.E. and proceed in the industry network that helps you progress and achieve goals you recommend. That's All Folks ☺ !!

RAMEL MAJETTE , ISIAH
C.E.O. Chief Executive Officer

Public Sources –

"Food Banks"
"Food Stamps"

"Thrift Stores"
And
"Good Wills"

Add Art surrounding: see page 48

Write how risk factor's has affected you "Ramel". In the past, then write how you "Ramel" will manage your risk factors in the future. –

Each risk factor affected me in a different way. <u>Major mental illness</u> is a risk factor. My mental illness causes me to be psychotic at times and this is a big focus of my treatment. Turns out I just have a chemical in balance and need to take medication to treat it. Another risk factor that has affected me in the past was <u>substance abuse.</u> Smoking marijuana was my hobby in life and I use it for self medication. Marijuana affected me negatively with the legal system and every time it became a cycle. That's why it's one of my risk factors as you read previously in my writing. Managing these risk factors in the future will be put into words simple but in action hard. Taking medication on my own every day at a particular time for the rest of my life is a hell of a responsibility. Staying away from marijuana is a challenge too , and I have a problem with it every time. Counseling and therapy will help most of my problems, but you can't force people to be perfect. But you can expect them to make smarter decisions for themselves.

*Upgrades Process Program on "PLUTO" –

Advance technology, best source of communication connection and quick reliable shipping and handling. All companions unite with "Planet Pluto World" progress and receive those benefits. The best personal PC equipment for each individuals and for members every year we can advance, renew and recycle the *Upgrade Process Program on "PLUTO".

*Everybody Ideas Gets Notice on "PLUTO"

(This is a policy) Creativity is the key concept of A.C.E. Associate dreams get shared. You can share what's ever on your mind at any given time and select what specific topic quote your ideas about. You can upload it to the network and that will set off alarms in other people's minds that are members. Then projects can be set-up and done then displayed to the public A.C.E. Associates Conquer Earth.

*PLUTO" –

Organization
       Classification
   Business Network.

Immaculate Clean!

*PLUTO's Biblica –

* New   World
Translation
Bible*

Giving

Back

To   the

Children   Around

The Universe!

Necessary

*Conclusion –

"PLUTO" decreasing the statistics in criminal act. Someone needs savior, with this organization people will not fear that temptation that there's no opportunity. No more or I'm too old to become somebody. My plan to unite people and we act professional to each other ideas and dreams then create life beautifully.   You can see all the possibilities how we can fight for better laws and health care and job opportunities. Things like that needs to be handed out not difficult to get. With A.C.E (Associates Conquer Earth) "United Power" we can look out for one another and pay each other back with respect and give credit of a good word about that particular associate. Decreasing criminal statistics is all about this website industry network, it's all about working together keeping each other out of trouble and print a perfect picture for the future. "PLUTO"

THE END

Background Summary –

Planet Pluto World Schizoaffective Vision!

Is about a network industry that is positive in so many ways and give a chance for A.C.E. associates to share their ideas, dreams, and goals and make it into a reality. This book is a guide to success mixed with my personal story. I share my true self and what I believe in to my readers. I hope you enjoy!

PLUTO